Violet Ideologies

Violet Ideologies

Poems by

David Wyman

Cover design by Shay Culligan

ISBN: 978-1-952326-61-5

Kelsay Books
502 South 1040 East, A-119
American Fork, Utah, 84003

For Caitlyn

Acknowledgments

I am grateful to the editors of the following publications in which these poems previously appeared. I'd also like to thank Caitlyn Wyman and Lori Lamothe for their help editing the manuscript.

The Aurorean: O, Manifesto

BlazeVOX: Violet Ideologies, Hegemony Of English, Euphoria Script, Talking To Myself On My Birthday, A Guest Of The Internationales; Re: Fishing, Saudade, Kohlinar, Murk Plectrum, First Things

Broadkill Review: Irish Laughter

Clockwise Cat: Ex 5 Icicle Dreamz

Dissident Voice: Ideal Gravity, Planet X, Listening To The End Of Time, Translated With Notes And Commentary, Last Days Of The Republic, Free-Form Throwing

Down In The Dirt: Scripted Voices

Dual Coast Magazine: Burnt Handwriting

Genre: Urban Arts: Magical Realms, Winner's Circle Horse Farm, Kayaking On The Fuyr River, Thunder Always Represents Divinity

Lotus-eater Magazine: Upstairs Dogs

Picaroon Poetry: Muzzle Flashes In The Dark

Squawk Back: The Happiest Of Beings

S/WORD: Beyond Our Arable Orb

Tuck Magazine: Evaporating Rivers, Unlike Words We Use To Speak To Babies

The Voices Project: Ambient Everywhere/Her, Learning the Math, Rise And Shine Dance

Zombie Logic Review: Ice Shelves, A Day With Fine Angles, Correlative Shadow Tone, Confiscate The Number 5, Talking Points: The Eies Of All People

Contents

THREE PLANET X SERIES

FOUR

You can't be suspicious of a tree, or accuse a bird or a squirrel of subversion or challenge the ideology of a violet.
—Hal Borland

Imagine no possessions
I wonder if you can
No need for greed or hunger
A brotherhood of man
—John Lennon

ONE

Violet Ideologies

Not how the world is is the mystical,
But that it is,
                    —L Wittgenstein

Let the poem as poems do talk about itself. Not what or how but
that. Resist a category of invented words chronologically culled by
the poet himself daubed in red ochre & rescued from syntax cradle
and all.

Warts appear then disappear spontaneously. I said I'm 'partly
Dave' too, a beast that wants discourse.

Anarchists! Question the flushing portrayal of people as skinny
beautiful wicked sexy frequently with such dexterity! I dreamt this
cruise was all-inclusive, that my dreams are all-inclusive, beyond
the picturesque representation of 'the glorification of randomly
common household objects.'

White leopard for avatar, active suitor. Later, cuttlefish for
breakfast, peacock sightings in Cancun, and the commercial being
an image of the sun's magnetic field. (But I get the feeling I've
copied this before.) Light, illuminate, enlighten

finagles its own trope. But every bad movie ends, Katarina.
Blogging is a great way to soothe your mind. Tomorrow's sunlight
gleams on white semantic fields. I try and break out of the funk
I'm in but Frank says, 'it has become our imagination, it has
become our power to envision…' By

the time they were both done running he gives the image and can
see his feet burning and he said the color red, said save me the
hectoring!

Evaporating Rivers

Water gives life to the 10,000 things
                                    —Lao Tsu

A river like a series of echoing
syllables, its greenish
gray stench, a city of blank
stares and a cause shaped
as a media narrative, back

when it was legal to dump
sewage and industrial waste
into rivers and
light them on fire.
                    A pre-industrial
vision turning sludge-filled
flows (oxygen-starved,
biologically dead) into clear
waters full of fish, turtles, mink,
otters, ospreys, increasing
property values—
a wild and scenic destination
promoting the power
to create change. We had become

consumers of ecological
miracles, planet-healers.

Now in a time when the movement
'lacks a unifying cause'
rivers are evaporating. Experts
are predicting water wars,
a future of scarcity. The *World*—

18

this is your card, here, but
reversed, meaning an end
to a cycle of life, tectonic
shifts. Lastly, an image of gasping
fish flip-flopping in hot mud—

Rise And Shine Dance

for my daughter, in her future

So the dancing is a cure, the drums wild
like movement in painting—
flashes of color equal
to the strife of future years, careless

of days going off the rails and
emptying into an evaporating atmosphere
or recurring, shaping
a kind of mimicry of motion and intent

that becomes the meme
by which others are recognized, awakening
to an even greater understanding
of the inner dimensional self—all this, but

what if there was more, beyond
these shifting shiny surfaces where
an ineluctable sea strips away the sand
and gathers us all up, like stars,

into the spoken word? The real cost
includes the risk of *not* having—in a future
where each day's a delight, where
music and dancing fill your house.

Menhaden Fish

Heads is eternity then. A syntax of light, sentences
in a bright cosmos and the real questions

keep repeating, an act of renewed forgetting.
Look to the East. The soul is hammered gold,

the market is *the* metaphysical force today!
As we die and our spirits move to another world,

our bodies dry up like these weeds so
we need to continue the process of making sure

that we are not one against the other
fleeing the suburbs with Blake's devil.

Some writing appears below but is not necessary.
Menhaden fish, 'typically used by fishermen as bait,

are a small, silver fish, whose oil is used
in vitamin supplements, lipstick and livestock feed.'

Ex 5 Icicle Dreamz

Footstep sound effects
marching stick figures
ideological containers
'manufacturing consent works
ceaselessly,' And my
cameo in a brief
filmic piece titled *My
Life or Transitive and
Intransitive,* a bio-pic.
Breathe alike wrinkles the
surface of time
easterly fermata, icicle dream,
number of winters—
wandering, thinking
No-sky fat
whirling flakes
and cold bites and
a scent, like
(having come this way before)
first snow—catching
Issa in translation,
wind full of names
ditch the referent
of who are imagined on screens
who flicker and are gone,
'though I with Death and
with reward did
threaten and encourage
him not doing 't
and being done,' endlessly
interactive a received
pronunciation. The window
behind him shows a
darkening sky, black

with silvery stars, then
a black curtain appears
to cover the window,
something falls from the sky.

Translated with Notes and Commentary

The face on the dust jacket keeps getting older.
Just now a shadow crosses my page and letters peel
in a piano-like sound
or a bird's whistle magnified to the height
of a crane displaying the *Resist* flag.
It's the grateful hours, the hours of gunfire and flies.
Images of home, its evasive circling, red roof
and this turning back, siphoning off daylight…
Still at least we're free. We have our freedoms.
Look how our enemies hate our freedoms.
(They will not be waiting for us long.)
O yeah, I can still see the bright purple nebula bursting
as I'm typing this here in a room on the event horizon.
Time itself is a bedraggled old sheriff
with half a swollen
gullet who plucks out green eyes only as I have argued.
The pace we set, institutional and ideological.
Our greater selves living explicitly in travel writing.

Unlike Words We Use to Speak to Babies

Hours are painted in glass.
Where we hedge our futures.
As Henry A Giroux said

(on *Moyers*) 'it's business
that really rules us now.'—We're
talking about falling in love

very fast, we're talking
to neutralize risk, we're
talking about commercial

media directing
our life goals. (Try
to clean up the blue

one piece at a time.)
Or about hippies, UFOs, Elon
Musk, AI, how the Koch

machine launders ideas
to a chirping public, where
the day's official transcript

gets redacted
in the celestial quiet
of TV. No, the tiger

that would eat you, it says,
hides a complexity
you don't need to know—

only staying connected
is what matters to them
making them totemic.

Free-Form Throwing

Dark money gives them
a megaphone in the public square. Look
what's going on behind,
what is ignored. Can a business
have a soul? Only those
men which have not the seal as
we have once again reminded
people that man is not free,
that man is made of clay.
Of an interior image
icebergs came to mind,
birds falling from the air.
They will awaken to this new time
with nothing to offer. Still
the land is ours, a gift—where
our identities clash creating
the freest capital markets,
the greatest liquidity
so let's not go overboard in setting and
enforcing tough emission
standards from man-made
sources (Reagan). Huge stone
monsters resistible as air
will tear open the earth—a real
political and ecological impact
on the failure of the world to act.
What the imagination, poetry,
can do in circumstances
that are somewhat oppressive
the analysis here is still a bit uneven.
'Whoever intentionally, willfully
and maliciously or wantonly,
paints, marks, scratches, etches or
otherwise marks, injures, mars,

defaces or destroys the real
or personal property of another
including but not limited to a wall—
shall be punished by imprisonment
in a state prison for a term
of not more than three years—

Ideal Gravity

What can be said of your company's spirit?
Its opportunities for
cost reduction? Its progress versus yesterday's

hurricane? The locus is not only this gesture
in the dark, where the hidden origins
of all poems are found out using variance analysis

on a night when ghosts march
against the assertion of what's being talked about, that
by doing more for the company

we're doing more for ourselves. This requires an adjustment
of course, a way of explaining where
the fences are, the mental chains, smoothing

it all out so it fits comfortably
like a net of discourse you can't throw off, identifying
the major contents of the annual business plan.

True Temples were Houses of Gods

The dead laid out on a hillside, including
letters making up the
words emmer and einkorn.

Evidence that the site had been covered
in ice, stone images
of wild game and bird species.

The idea is a future
archeology
analyzing artifacts from our present.

Eight feet down deposits discovered
in a 'chilly muck' turned
out to be a trash dump aligned

to the summer solstice and containing
plastic waste; Z arguing
objects cannot be identified

without all the data in context.
No signature of machine intelligence
at either level. Figure 2.9

at one end of a long table, in front of a pile of bones,
radiation levels spiking. Z offered
alternative descriptions,

the find signifying a cult of consumption
or cult of death. Tested high for
radioactive contamination, wild animals

returned with early effects
of mutation even glowing. Looming
megaliths indicating a later but

more primitive settlement.
Images of high-flying
carrion birds transporting

the flesh of the dead up
to the heavens countering arguments (Z et al.)
against it being a temple complex.

A Day with Fine Angles

That voice on the radio upstairs hints
at a way to make sense of lines
that have the eerie, seductive
ring of the inevitable. Hype
washes it away, the signal, a kind of

tangent, circular in its flight
across these gilded skies
in a time when fact will strike the reader
as superfluous. But how
can you tell right now which one,

standing out there on the ledge,
wants to be saved and which one
wants to fly? The sacralizing mind's
on fire all the time
like hot glass blown full of air—

and yet again we're forced to trust
the description as being accurate
and we're unlikely to know
where it is not. But the idea that some of *our* words
are missing or might've been erased

disturbs us, keeps us up all night
and away from the snowier summits
of consciousness that we've somehow
exchanged for this game, where
our trajectories almost almost intersect.

Paradise

Voices in a cold light, the bass like
a deep haze on a road rising
like the tone of a question and now
a looser feeling, its novelty

waking (working) in a variable space
while the other side
looks at sales figures all day long
convinced the next line

is intentional. I lay awake
till morning redolent as a flow chart.
These ambitious annotations,
files scheduled for revision,

a dirty orange autumn, its quirky
ending with the future of
the book in doubt and us here
less open to ecstatic discoveries…

Does he know who you are, who I am?
The prosier baggage doesn't work
unless you view it as truly,
competently lyrical. A last last word.

Gonzalo's Cry

8. Idleness proverbially begets lust.
Write the world is not far enough.
A fresh doublet, a ship wrecked

on an island full of stray noises
an island of scripted voices—
Then Gonzalo's cry, 'For no kind

of traffic' (commerce)
'No sovereignty'
An island caged in the ribs

of a wrecked ship, beaming
with the joy of an infant
whose face is a Guy Fawkes mask,

kaleidoscopic; the sprite
in the form of a CGI 'floating
across solid surfaces

taking on multiple forms…'
Then Greenblatt on Montaigne
'giving an account of himself'—

Mocking Gonzalo mocking Montaigne
as authorial intent—
an honest old counsellor's

euphoria begets a proto-anarchist
utopia, based in nature,
laughingly represented,

an imaginary island's polysemic
location, appearing
at least once in the Arctic, in ice—

where, had they wrecked 1800 miles
south of Bermuda[1], Gonzalo
might've discovered it for real…

---

[1] The Piaroa, a highly egalitarian society living along tributaries of the Orinoco
which ethnographer Joanna Overing herself describes as anarchists. David
Graeber

Talking Points: The Eies of All People

Yes, they got it all teed up—
glass shattering, the eies...
Up passed the layers of city architecture
reflected in a glass tower.

Thus mere light is pleasing to the mind.
A shiny city upon a hill shining
like it does in movies or on the news,
stronger than oceans, built

soe that the riche and mighty
should not eate upp the poore...
The word stock of urban life,
its shrill heat and crowd noise,

a single thronging unified
in one augmented reality
like the radiant nostalgia of the olde ballpark.
In the verbatim transcript, it says

nor the poore and dispised rise
upp against and shake off theire yoake.
A tall, proud city humming commerce...
Today the eyes of all people are truly—

5 Lucky Lobsters

The nakedest after-party dresses on the red carpet.
Counting them is one way to combat insomnia.
Gunshots of happiness, gunshots of joy,
the vigilante's forked tongue licking
our rancid history
like its fellow traveler, like a slice of venison.
Insert obsolete 60s slang here.
Our days dwindling like the number
of monarch butterflies wintering in Mexican forests—
skywriting ominous music in the background—
a ghostly dualism, heavy spirals of snow.
This describes his own birth as he remembers it
as a kind of falling
off or falling as, in space
in no recognizable direction, left or up…
No, the question is—what has to happen
to make this stop? Worldbuilding
billionaire oligarchs
inventing a totally logical history,
including lots of peasants,
a winter storm's gunshots like a non-denial denial,
wind patterns shifting unexpectedly
across our continent, the view
of the city from the sky freezing over.
Alternately everyone is free.
And everyone is aware of what the sign,
impossible to recreate by hand,
a kind of spoken calligraphy,
becomes, like an inverted coastline.
Here a separateness to things, held in orbit, profusely,
the 10,000 things that are brought forth
to make the world again, rising
in colorful creation for a new dance.
It assumes the burden of proof lies on them (Chomsky).

Here we're all diehard fans of Sakara.
Here corn is a metonym for human.
Here too we may never know where we have been.
Here you're supposed to crumple it, light it up.

Winner's Circle Horse Farm

What made us laugh. I know what you will say
the last time we meet.

Said this new doctor, from China,
had been right about her fertility.

Sounds (like sh + ch)
are added where they don't appear

and when I talk I don't open my mouth.
Testing life against legend.

We walked to a farm owned
by a near-celebrity. Horses

stared at us as if in trance.
Each new facial expression *is* a new face.

Said she feared she might have weak chi.
And how early the heart develops in a fetus.

Going back we followed a stone wall
zigzagging decoratively

down a stubbled hillside. Then a guy on a bridge
catching a silver fish—

First Things

It's like dark matter, it's hard to see it but it's messing with the gravity of things. This is that title line expressing a luxurious gloom, our melancholic nostalgia for what has

not yet happened, its colors the colors of Edvard Munch. To promote for us a new formula for being, 'experts in national security couldn't fail to notice that 43 percent of respondents had an actual defined view on bombing a place in a cartoon.' Next then the burning

of books, a process for pressuring anyone to do anything.

Ideas go unchallenged. First things likens

unrelentingly ersatz futures. Just knowing how your debts will be treated after you're gone signifies—what? *That* to a people who had a special love of faith, freedom and peace, who tried to inoculate the Indians by means of blankets, a divine plan. Label that language sculpture. A huge whirling storm of possible events, wobbly timelines, a future trying to crystallize out of the streaming present. Someone like Jesus might convince them. Don't hesitate to pick up small objects, such as a tennis ball, and throw them at coyotes. Lennon said, 'The only thing they don't know how to handle is non-violence and humor.' Pretend we all think the same. Your transaction ID for this payment is: 5PM611573D574571K.

How to Play the Violin

The lines split off. Here breaking in shards
or evenly as flaxen
hair, a statement about ecology
and the word minuets
for minutes. On the next page the word zephyr
is crossed out and the noise
comes from a heart monitor. Clouds
in the painting represent the life
of the mind, a daydream. Air
and light seep in. It all ends in a slogan.
And some guy sitting in the bleachers
on a higher step to watch the game
alone might have a purpose here too.
The line continues along
with the high sustain of notes forming
a diminished chord. A broken
stone is a barrier. Weeds
are growing around it and no one
will have the energy to get rid of them
till morning. Sight is a factor in elegance.

O

Found interiors like tides of ice.
A light snow unafraid
of signification covering open fields.

Invisible scaffoldings like hidden meanings
flash innocuously.
Till it comes unraveled. So.

What *is* given over? Lured away
by these lights, by this signaling
like a hand rising up

in the shape of a hand, in a shape
like many hands
rising up—the O as in

O speech! O revolution! O baby!
encrypted in a coded night,
in this fiery precariousness, in us?

TWO

Muzzle Flashes in the Dark

Hours before the ice age is scheduled to begin,
the evening percolates with wistful faces.

The masks are fixed, images representing
things we don't want but they stick

even when being two separate persons
can keep you from losing a sense of self.

And the streets act like we don't belong.
A sign advertising *Psychic Readings* alludes

to our higher aspirations, but
with so many discredited terms—

none of this ever gets us anywhere.
As always we look forward, parts of an idea

affecting the unlettered future. Better
to move away then, not be stuck to a place,

keep it in the camouflage of dreams
that wake you up in the night, as I have

no feel for where I stand right now, the answer
deferring to a brighter probability of days.

Wildflowers in a Glass

A timeline can be a way of organizing
but what about all the in-betweens?
Here it appears in a representation
introducing a noted yet active aesthetics—

Here's a fine-spun re-working, purer
with all its imperfections, a vision under
glass, like a utopian future
where we've finally learned to stop

using money, where new ideas
are possible. But today we're on a kind of loop
looking not out of a window at snow but
at a picture of someone looking out a window

at snow, ad infinitum, as it all flows, flowing
to where every man must be free
to become whatever God
intends he should become, not

that every man must be level...
Remember, you are usually introverted
when it comes to people
but you can also easily be the center

of attention when you want?
Just copy it and read it—it doesn't mean
what it meant, moving as one continued
vision, a unity of what is broken.

Upstairs Dogs

Say this. We hope that you will confirm it exceeds your expectations. Like figures in a group sculpture, still the only clue. Guffaw, guffaw, their wings are gossamer. On earth the color change is inaudible and probably too lofty. I can watch this maybe one more time but I'm not really anonymous anymore. Bubbles coming out of the clown's mouth were hieroglyphics and we knew we could read them, but silently at our desks. Here the real sky hangs like a loose tarp. Do you know when someone *is* watching you? Meandering is how it came out, referring to the glaze.

Various sayings and so many angels sorting out petitions written on voluminous paper sheets and scraps from people all over the world. What can be heard is *in* the walls. Swim is the verb. Do not walk barefoot on hot surfaces. Some of the old whales choose to stay in the northern sea. Why do I dream this, that I'm not welcome in the house? Like unnecessary *italics,* we joined for just one day. Say he ponders quite eloquently about the entirety of the journey. And the elevator regularly continuing, continuing without stopping. Then. An opening, but no sound, no wind, no words, nothing.

High Quality Mornings for Less

1

Beyond, the rows are straight across and can
be read either way, left to right or right

to left, but talk is a synonym for action.
The cracks in these stone walls are a kind of tell;

some morning glories are 'excellent vines
for creating summer shade on building walls

when trellised, thus keeping the building cooler
and reducing heating and cooling costs.'

I have lived both lark and night owl, as well
as witnessed a lark and night owl in action, so

yes, we need to be *sure* our voice is always heard.
(It is OK to say, this is what I want—and go for it!)

An unthinkable event puts things into perspective.
We apologize for any delay this may cause you.

2

Our flat provincial sky, studded with balloons.
Tourists out photographing the foliage,

offering this observation, scouting out the herd,
revolutionizing everything. Signals coming

in from every angle as if from cosmic space
but these outlier designs

are too ridiculous for mass consumption.
A word beginning with the letter *A* is lost.

Its book is a feral cat.—That wood carving
over the altar said, 'He taught us how to fear God.'

Of course, but each thing must correspond or all
we end up with are trinkets from the gift shop.

Unraveling as it goes, all we have is this shiny surface.
The hype is mostly in hoping to see some skin.

Correlative Shadow Tone

On the eve of the Mayan Apocalypse,
Bak'tun 13, 12/21/12

On the day before the day it all ends
there's no waiting. Snow
swirls sideways in parentheses with us
(here) immersed in the wonder
as if a new word was about to be spoken.

The word, its horizon continually
and unevenly moving away, intimate
wreckage, characters
in hieratic white space fracturing—
this is what we have, many lives

but most are unlived
or lived by someone else. Negative
beliefs can, by default, cast what you don't like.
Unless the glass is opaque,
the glint only a figment, then nothing.

Say, we breathed this soot
and formed ourselves from it, say
in a universe of no delete ducks and mimes.
Part of a line coheres behind us.
Tonight, there's no escaping the frame.

Confiscate the Number 5

They make it speak differently, ad hoc.
Jangling new coins in their mouths like that

sounds like hear or there. Like a bleep.
Seven across: cracked the famous Houdini code.

They made it speak with little to no punctuation.
Yes, and picked all the best nouns in public

but not hollyhocks, lavender or wheat.
This, says confiscate the number 5. You

say it and the saying makes it true
such as the word vector meaning

like a tic, or how there can be many even
when the word looks singular, which is

also felt when it is heard. The semantic
range of "Forget your best adventures"

makes no sense. All quotations are approximate.
Like marks on a screen too blurry to be read—

Ten years is long enough to wait. (Tic or tick?)
In the mirror, the candle is white and remains lit.

Hegemony of English

Money is speech, SCOTUS

What the hegemony of English sounds
like, according to one COO, 'ad
load will play a less significant
factor driving revenue forward.' That
to stimulate meaning/value—
as it could provide the color for how
one sees the world (Whorf). Where
in translation, risky as it is,
the soft parts may be gutted out like
with oysters. In a vision I keep seeing stars
falling from the sky and people running—
protests, unrest, stress in the population—
the sign of infinity (not sure what it means)
fires, more images of drought, no
snow where there should be snow—
a caterpillar dissolving into liquid as
the unraveling of the old system. It's
like, every day, you can't believe this is happening,
where 'neo-liberal oligarchs
get to keep raking in the cash with their
ecocidal war-
mongering exploitation.' Here it also means
a spiritualized process, one
we internalize that makes us who we are not
just manufacturing things we can sell. But
then we are more interested
in the performance than in whether
it's true, aren't we, it says as
a printer's devil crosses
the half-lit stage, muttering. It's
never quite possible to hear
what he's saying but he's the key.
He knows something. But someone

pulls his beard, flicks his face—
OK so where does this go?
He knows something. Shit
yeah, he knows we're doomed. So

what are we going to save on next?
It's true we share a common
corporate language
which is, after all, what we have
to close a deal. But our words still
slide along edges and disappear
like notes, scoffed up in that vacancy
of air, its eddies moving
almost at right angles to us. Pinker
cites 'an ingenuous study on
the mental life of infants,' suggests
a comparison to monkeys but
for the moment we're stuck
in a whirling phonological loop, our
prisonhouse, the austere
limits of an austere world. And in that
shadowed against a burning sky
a flea. Tremble at the voice
heralding us in our
international language, fluent
and deterministic,
a cacophony—all of that species
'grinning and snatching…' its sound
like coins crashing—Blake's Hell
is a verbal possibility too, an unstable
isotope, elusive as an unmarked grave.

Spoken Word

This time words taste like hard cider.
They linger
like haze in the cool
of a pub redolent

with sheer magnification. It's like that.
A free play. Unsupervised
time to improvise in our scripted
lives, the sense of

victory deflating later in dark gusts.
I dreamt all night, first
about my father's labors and then
that I was here

lost in a cruel bureaucratic plot,
scuffling about,
bootless, not finding the room
till someone opened a door

and kindly pointed. Now, groggy,
kinda pissed, I'm following
the same traffic (again) to where the
wind bluntly blows me off my feet.

A First Syllable of Value

Echoes or in silence. The vocal was something
they really really

wanted to control. A twiggy or tricky
phrase to parse

when so many have lost their currency. A cloud
sprinkling fertilizing rain

on fields of ripe sentences.
As the fear factor is removed

prices retreat rather quickly, he said aloud.
So my vocal presence has been.

What you get are living breathing poets—
to rattle you awake,

media tastemakers specializing
in selling you an image you're dying

to consume, a first syllable of value.
The key word to underline was *belies*.

Is it earned? This optimism like melting ice?
The loon in the pond laughs out loud.

Burnt Handwriting

Trail rocks—wet leaves, talk—
determined footing, no
view yet but a cell tower
at the top, the world as a work of—

This one means transience
like a vagrant—
One day—sans home, sans money (possessions)
freed from this—but

all assets finally seized
with the wind…or this,
it accumulates meanings, borrows—it means
temples of enlightened beings

who speak, write, sign
in what gets termed an ideal language
you can't rush through, sample
but kind of have to leave it whole.

I made it morning she once said,
the baby bouncing in her crib.
Then a way out. Burnt beyond, the world
just wishes, the mystical mind, a garden—

Ambient Everywhere/*Her*

A screen glows then is silent.
The mystical mind, a garden…
'You will be safe, you will be warm.'
Shadows multiply behind

dancers. A voice with an accent,
as an alarm goes off, says don't
get up, someone will be in there shortly,
don't get up. —Then a face

like a rubber mask, snarls.
A gold shade whips across,
moves as if through vertical space
with strength and ease and grace

as in electronic textures and
no persistent beat: you will be safe.
In a dance of perfect stillness.
The world is full of images,

some of them will be transparent.
The neighbors see everything.
The neighbors are (always) watching.
Be careful, it might dry like that.

Many Rooms

Vivified, our description of
the desert imagination,

having conceived. What's
going on in that converted space
we call the afterlife?
(It's raining assiduously.) Next,

call these sky mansions
'placeholders
of value.' We read into it
money, obols over our eyes,
yet as a kid standing, staring
at two figures
in the wood cut over
the alter, who hastened
my dissonance, my dissidence. So
do you have a theory
on how it happens? Naming it
in a way that precludes
knowing it?

The way is prepared for you, *proceed
to the route.*
    The description sort of
comforts the believers while
at the same time
it reinforces the power
of the hierarchy
here where the church
tower's crumbling after 126 years.

The lanes of the cemetery
lead to a distant country,
unworldly joy. Consoled
by a musicality of phrases, phrases
of transport. This conceit

like a second sun
where you are
continuously now. Or you are
where I am. Or this is you?
In a cold country?
                  The wind hurts.
It's hard to breathe and
your hands sting, *#proceed to the route—*

Kayaking on the Fuyr River

These new strings sound like the word cascade
and suddenly I'm the one going over the waterfall
on the last day of boating on the Fuyr River, when
the kayak became pinned in the rocks trapping
us under the deep surging water. Despite
our best efforts to free ourselves, we quickly realize
we're not in control of our futures. Out of reach,
with literally minutes left to register the nows
in our consciousness, and the world
turning a paler shade of red, we let the idea
of death go altogether, and a face turns up but
not the one expected. Only one idea
is perfectly true, says the kid bedazzled by the mystery.
But which one? It takes a long time
to get an answer back but then a voice
shouting over the intercom says, 'you will not fully
understand this, since you will not be familiar
with the academic debates to which they refer.'
And it's right. Whether they're trying to look sexy
or doing their best to pretend they're too cool
for school, some stars never flash
their pearly whites for the cameras, do they? Just
as summer's never what I think it's going to be.

Finish Elements

A flat sun dot-perfect and long
enough for silence—
A cardinal red as April 19th whizzing by
like a jet hurtling in sidelong space—

then like a message from my father
who died two years ago…
The noun quotidian here
feels out of place and the blurb

describes a kind of speech no one
could wear, not even inside out
as it was meant to be read. (They say
he opts for a longer line and it shakes.)

Parts of it are not the same but if you still need more space,
attach separate statements
that are the same size as the printed schedule.
Said she agreed, there being no afterlife.

Irish Laughter

for my mother

Irish laughter, breaking glass,
and where you are now. Perhaps
in this book?

In the words 'a figure
glided quietly from
bed to bed,
smoothing a blanket,
settling a pillow,'
every night
naming each of us
in your prayers? About

4:36 AM, I see you on my couch.
A firefly, whispering love
as a tonic to adversity.

This only days after the Super
Blood Moon
lunar eclipse…Souls

of the dead sometimes return to us
as birds. Like your two cardinals did.

But when I step out into the cold now
the trees are birdless.

It's your laughter we've come to hear.
It's the light, in all of our rooms.

Learning the Math

for Caitlyn

Yellow, bright as a rain jacket—
and the gray shiny rain.
Time, a game of *Pico, Fermi, Bagel*
but at such a speed

like that bus that never stopped
and then how you held numbers
in your hands, tiny
fingers multiplying among stars—

And those in-betweens, the dance
like everything we ever said.
Words, as breath itself.
I thought of April snow and the sky

as a shimmering screen
where everything is saved,
first days, first steps, first words—
in the calculus of stretching space.

THREE PLANET X SERIES

1~The Happiest of Beings

Today all this blue is wild and the urban coyote—
the blood moon, songs sung to infants, all digital

media, even the sound of a train far off
either distant or in memory, are wild

as untaxed capital gains, beyond our commodified
speech, wild as the joker and the suicide king,

riotous and nocturnal, innocently corybantic.
What are the syllables, the visible forms,

the happiest of beings? I wake in the night too
in fear of what my daughter's world might be...

John 10:30 (KJV) I and my father are one?
Verses show their argument to be false

and the cult of the book as authoritative.
Does this say wood drake instead of duck for a reason?

All the evidence turns out to be passages. When
it falls on impermanence instead I too am free...

2 ~ Listening to the End of Time

The book then is your authoritative guide,
its words like gestures in the dark,

its passages masquerading as proofs
of the indisputable in hieratic script. But here

the translation is uncertain: this word
is most often translated as *time,* as in

the impossible lifting its right hand to heaven
saying, 'there shall be time no longer...'—That

in exchange for the 'gentlest apocalypse imaginable
whose rhythms swing along in intricate patterns

without ever obeying a regular beat.' Time
beaten on a drum is eradicated in this piece

composed, while Messiaen was under guard, for
himself (piano), Pasquier (cello), Akoka (clarinet)

and Le Boulaire (violin). In 1976, the group Tashi
recorded the definitive version on the RCA label.

3 ~ Agnostic Blue

A parallel blue sky of the mind, a reason.
Heaven as a progressive hue.

In the conflagration, the magnetic erasure of world data.
We are all allegory and pomp.

A life under or all blue, cheap gasoline and
the discourse of prophecy

to make its point. A replica of a replica.
Like this one that determines how we read it.

Yet, I could follow it up to the standing stones set
at angles to the solstices

and even a little farther off, in time.
Where the wild is a construct there we venture.

Insistently I wanted to take it all in, all home, but
the problem of a god or afterlife is trickier.

It was mine already, all I had to do was say. Here
where we are never not on camera anymore…

4 ~ Gospel of Mary

Here is the million-dollar question: will you
go to heaven when you die?

The dialogue invites the reader inward in
the direction of the text, its authority

not always resting on evidence. (Ehrman
uses the term "pseudepigrapha.")

Here it says those who seek for it will find it.
Right at this point we're missing four pages.

Anyone with two ears should listen. Upset
that he would reveal himself to a woman—

she's describing how the soul can ascend
and escape its material trappings here on earth…

Be silent and submissive, hanging by
their hair, and what else was kept from you—

the end of days occurring in our time in all times.
Suffering makes more sense in a godless world.

5 ~ H+

After a while it seems to change direction like
the effect zebra stripes have on a lion, like

spokes, like an atheist converting
on his deathbed. But we all want to be close to them,

celebrities, stand in long lines in bad
weather, consumed. For now this illusion of monologue

is a kind of wood-shedding. But monologue
is partly correct as is a sense of self,

a word problem. I said, still I doubt
I'll live long enough to upload myself

into a cloud, sign of a failed Gnosticism. Too
didactic. It says here, I had in mind a river

crossing to no fixed point, an oblique reference
to the five who turned away (sans footnote) and

a theory about the inevitability of the light, a note
saying how an unknown number of lines are lost…

6 ~ Ice Shelves

Ice shelves set to break apart in high definition.
The universe as two-dimensional hologram.

Light glinting frantically off and on
the wrinkled surface of a pond, the names

of things appearing in subtitles while
visiting the text in a dream of an ideal language.

Its words are English, the language is not.
What makes it ideal is its perfect clarity,

how it reveals to us exactly *why* we make
our consumer choices in a world ablaze

with freedoms, where the definition
of talent is being true to yourself, where legends

live on among accolades and superlatives
and continue to inspire and show us what's great…

So instead of noise, constellations of sound,
uncanny pronunciations, like dreaming in color.

7 ~Scrying Out Loud

Objects like talk. What the score is depending
on so many words, the players

glossing existence in a dignified sentence
where no number is given. A greedy

or rapacious person's distensible throat pouch,
long neck. A sound behind,

like corpusants: lake to being, the word quest for
composing a social or political movement.

Like Jehu they march voting to cause us harm;
where the truth of an idea is not

the primary reason for its acceptance, discover
how you can rapidly start speaking

with only a few remaining redactions.
The removing process like evening prose, light

through an inner open space or cavity radiating
equally in all directions. Bleats, but like an adverb.

8 ~ Planet X

Today we are free or living in the Matrix.
A foothold for people of conscience

to remain silent. The post said, 'the mythical
Planet X is real and scientists are calling it

Planet Nine.' You are there too walking along
its highly elongated orbit, walking

while keeping in mind what can't be measured
in this agnostic blue. Walking and whistling

a bootleg version of, first, whale-song then
that *Beatles* tune 'Happiness Is A Warm Gun.'

Nothing says well-traveled like a worn trunk.
Words like oxygen for the soul freely

chosen from the codes of others, decorating
fearless with no rules, here where

the plans for you are known, where you step
into a painting on a carpet that defines the space.

FOUR

FOUR

Saudade

Including large contributors whose names
appear on public buildings,
we too wonder what it will be, this substituting

fresh adjectives for our displaced
lyric selves literally changing
how the days turn out for us the way

syntax choreographs thinking. Turns out
that Mallarme quote, 'Speech is no more
than a commercial approach to reality,' says it all.

Nomadic here is defined by a Bedouin,
his face covered, in a violent sandstorm
moving horizontally away and

drifting like 'textually aborted
vectors at a time of copulative semantics
and huge displacements'

seen as on a screen suspended, made of light.
Will the mysterious shadow planet Nibiru
obliterate Earth in October?

There's a bourgeoisie of poets too. They
diagram sentences talking in their sleep, sotto
voce and all at once, like a chorus.

Yet at least two of us dreamt of the Roman fasces
representing our fear of the future
in a time of spiritual reckoning,

but in our virtual sunsets on red beaches
wee the people, we will be free.
Here let me quote the greatest movie of all time:

as the dread pirate Roberts from
The Princess Bride said 'Life is pain, highness.
Anyone who says differently is selling something.'

That is, because the commodification of the self
requires strict scrutiny,
a constant rebranding. This allows their energy

to flow easily after externals
as their inner lives aren't calling for attention.
After breakfast then, a demonstration sabotaged

by the president's goons. Tanks
rolling down Fifth Avenue at high noon.
Streets on fire tonight at eleven.

Title note: 'a vague and constant desire for something
that does not and probably cannot exist' (Bell).
Hierarchies of angels sing thee to thy sleep.

Talking to Myself on My Birthday

Who is speaking in this way?
—R Barthes

In the end it makes you spectral, diffident and cool.
However the ruling astrological planet for this particular day
      is Mercury.

Blank pages indicate a return to mindfulness.
The imaginary mark (or marks) acting as a guide.
Its exteriority lit only here and there by Christmas lights.
Next a diminishing figurine ambling along a shoreline not
focused on anything. Gulls coming into view and
the blue of the planet as seen from space…

The great turning begins in earnest.
We are working toward providing enough
connectivity next week to satisfy
taking away the occasion for speaking,
the voice. The effect is real but
the photo only captures water, ionized air.

The blue of the planet as seen from space fading, days
the color of factory brick
but no windows no doors. It's useless to look
for an exit, beyond filtered perceptions or the sense
of having seen it on TV, to a place somehow
miraculously freed from commercial development,

its bright horizon extending infinitely like the soul—
its big-screen adaptation 'glossy, well cast and a consistent hoot.'
Toast sesame seeds in coconut oil over medium heat.
Check less interest in things you used to enjoy.

Landscape is temporary too. They said, it seemed hip
in the sixties, a state of pure exchange—mill to
mall and gun for fun. Into which you fall continually
disappearing, at last becoming spectral. Like de Vere.

Scripted Voices

An oboe concealing Planet X in sirenic melodies.
Where we believed in the reign of fire and chaos.
Till Shakespeare murdered sleep.
Filling out forms simply may silence gunfire.
Our movement lacking erotic zeal,
our movement creeping backward, whistling,
running from aliens, Blue Meanies & drones...
Who said only the police can tell if we're lying?
Who said they saved Planet X electronically?
Their scripted voices wailed, your tea's ready.
The villain is always winter. This
is where the nine who never sleep are welcomed
onto the wreck where they become weightless.
O, we have witnessed space stretching like nylon.

Euphoria Script

How to sum it up then, their candid jabber,
the glass changing every time you look at it,
those objects we dreamt of

made of ivory, marble and rare woods accessible
only to the rich. The play of ideas—otherwise known
as inspiration—is one of the amazing things

about working with others, rising
in colorful creation for a new dance of awakening…So—
Take a million selfies. Look relatable. Is it because I *am*

a public person, a conceit, a bit of left-hand English?
Fleeting yet held onto as a fiction, I said I am this weather.
Scripted lives caught on tape making a zigzag for the exit—

dark backward, blend and clash, fallin' down like hail,
yet I have crossed safely over
via platitudes or prophecies exerting my hands and feet.

Ignoring trolls is always the best way to go, unless
you're going to pull a Steve Nash. We always encourage that.
Find strength within you and be kind to yourself.

We are here to serve a population from real
to imagined that can seem ungrateful.
—Tired of owning junk? Insert trendy electronica here.

O, I might harp on trivial issues but nowadays
I try to stay as positive as possible,
I want the haters to know my life is fantastic.

(Still why do I dream *this,* that I'm not welcome in the house?)
Yeah, I understand some of its meaning even
if I know there can be many meanings in this prophecy,

'a paradigmatic figuration, as in the force
of the composition is paradigmatic of strategies
of inter-disciplinary reading,' generally, like

the temporary value a poem provides, the ability to just
walk around (outside) and let the breeze kind of rush over,
a buoyancy in old age, like a kind of design.

Deity Syllables

It is said that seeing one, especially one
as it's being made,
is enough—a tracing out of shapes

then color, of its lettering and deity
syllables, its perfect form and balance—
a two dimensional

sign of a temple
that will become the translucent
shape of a mind, whose

sign is also transience, like this—
like actual letters of the
word-in-sand, where there is one world

but where its syllables are removed
and in a certain order—Though here
a prose fragment, turned on its side, juts out—

Like chemicals absorbed into the bloodstream
found language finds
its way in to the brain as potentially

harmful substances are common
in foods we eat, especially
foods stored in plastic containers—

Investing In The Azure Tint

Cue fanfare: 'The Call to the Post.'
High angle shot of the field—cut
to number 3
overtaking the lead,
leaps—then freeze
close-up on the horse,
its eyes & nostrils flared.

Announcer: 'How will you know
what is enough?' (Music swells.)

—Here, you are the innovative
maverick. A true horse of instruction
you are your performance,
the edge
in a competitive market.

Featured you become like sage,
a world in a garret,
spinning thrilling glorious hours
reflected in windows
of a poor house in a rich universe—

or like other shadowy
superfluities
where money's not required,
the ultra sassy,
like the malt-flavored nougat like
any image you're dying
to consume—Go!
Sell your clothes!
It's good to have heroes!

Our aims must be the same
where money *is* required,
where only God
will see you which is not meant
to suggest actual or
expected fees all of which may vary
(though 'you are not your own,
you were purchased at a price'...)

Today we celebrate a new age
of celebrity worship,
encoded in our DNA—Evolutionary
biologists say,
as hunting is not now an essential skill,
as it was in prehistoric times, we
look to celebrities
whose fame and
fortune we wish to emulate
integrating ourselves
into that hierarchy
as spectators, bank clerks—

In Chromatic Weather

Old stake of winter resistance &
this siphoning off
of daylight. Imagining clacks
and claps of chopping wood,

an act like stepping quickly
into frame. Signing, we
arrive on Ferris Wheels, riders
of a cresting wave, insurgents

of seasonal convictions blandly
transmogrified into copyrighted
catchphrases. Worn hearts
turn meaning into value. Even

at velocities where time turns into
space, charity is
a means. Reflecting what a
headless hierarchy bestows but—

it just sounds like an ad. Winter's
intimate polemic, its unsettling
calm, here where to redeem
the sign still requires exact change.

Magical Realms

Whorls of light then static, voices
like new strings like
chimes signaling a future of
trivial privacies, lost sightings, the sky's

artificial flavorings. Can I say then
this echo's universally
a rejection of voice?
They're silent now, absorbed
in the light of a numinous world
whose map is lost. Then exists in legend.
Then not at all. But the sky's
nearly legible. Here it says inhale
what you believe or just
inhale, breathe. In time entropy

devours us, a sound
like helicopter blades: 'Fantasy still
speaks to us though, so it doesn't matter
if it's an elf or a dwarf
in those magical realms, you
can make a difference.'

         And even now
digging through the trash
before the trucks come to haul away
what can't be reinvented,
there's a tingling of familiarity
but an unassailable need
to read on. Till the book explodes

in your hands. Fire is a substitute,
in an age of plastic idols,
for our memory of the earth
but only speech can create a world.

At World's End Tavern (irl)

So the idea of this as continuous, out
where there are tracks already
only when it catches up to where
I am now it's, like, five in the morning. This

is where reading about sailing to that sacred city
is the same as going there,
an eminently reasonable
'supramundane goal,' a theatrical defense

of the mind's habitual curving away
till a consensus emerges
around the impact of real-time social experiences
on driving user behavior. Just right

click the NPC to see the quest text,
read it, and then click "Accept"
to accept the quest…Me,
I'm a wanderer by nature

but now I'm just exhausted with it—
I need to stop repeating
drifter cycles in this life, wait for the music,
relax and learn to receive

wise and happy thoughts
from every part of the universe. Spirit
is absence, a fixed binary.
But it's right, for an old man. Till the quest

becomes increasingly ironic. Just keep
the power of your toon
relatively toned down
and watch out for creatures

with red-colored names—
they're aggressive and will attack
if you get too close. Then other enemies
in the area may join in against *you*.

Salem

Old ties to that glittering world, only this ephemeral
art installation made of thousands
of woven saplings, whimsically exploring—but

not these comic book heroes or that popular cyborg
who greeted us for lunch at the Flying Saucer Pizza Co—
after a morning spent hunting witches,

the nineteen who were hanged here
based on spectral evidence, in this village
full of cool shops selling Celtic runes, psychic

readings, enchanted chocolates, T-shirts, magic
wands in a perfect replica of
Ollivanders on Diagon Alley. The day was bright.

One actual place named in a famous school book
materialized here too, around
the corner in the glare, on Derby Street…

The day was bright, with just the 'illusion
of three-dimensional space, rhythmic motion
and the glow of projected light' exactly

like olde Hollywood in that gigantic Thomas
Hart Benton poster unfurled at the entrance
of the Peabody Essex Museum. —God help me!!

But there's still the unanswerable—do you know,
shouts the heckling troll, that the majority of atheists
on their death beds cry out saying God help me??

All art is made of this, and life. The mystical is the real.
So says the bat, hairless and frantic—
now circling the TV room, the kitchen—colliding—

Thunder Always Represents Divinity

Like a fossil embedded in a rock, there is something there
but at an angle where his English sounds
the way I imagine Rilke's German must sound
though I've only read him in translation. So...
'What is this riddle language mystics speak?'

A kind of hermetic signification takes over from here
and suddenly we know what everything means, like how
they want to eat in a way that feels more natural
and authentic to them, as some have claimed to be affected
by the earth's wobble and its loss of magnetic energies
typical of a later phase.
                                        Things like the 'forced solitude
of the mind against the cool blankness
of an object world' are resolved by the sudden force
of poetry, even with our tendency to confuse the poet
with this unitary expressive self, its resplendent I.

Spectral Evidence

A cartoon anarchist, our freedoms, the idea of artificial
personhood, a world of canned answers and especially the idea of
having to be 'impossibly thin pretty and flawless but act as if it
takes no work,' the soul like a turbo shot of espresso (Free! Limit
one coupon per customer) a name that is not a name—just an
inverse like things falling up, beyond the red lines of morning,
summoning birds to those trees whose secrets live a thousand years
wrapped up and forgotten like the tongue used to invoke charms—
where two boring characters exchange wooden dialogue under a
sky with no holes, their chaos of radical enjambment, and what
gets left here—us, fusting about like this with only an inkling of
our commodified salvation stored up in folded hands, while music
that is meant to be heart-stirring plays on a soundtrack very
loudly—

A Guest Of The Internationales

In a dream called *A Guest of the Internationales*
my ideal house appears
on a green hillside
on an island. It's white
eco-friendly brimming
with natural light—
but when I go out in the world
everything
presents itself at once, everything
is displayed
as if it were all on sale. Turns out

materialism restores
dignity
               and
intellectual
integrity   with

easy-to-perform (sublime)
mysteries
            though
        it can take the form
of a spiritual
        consumerism
        tailored
to one's own unhealthy
individualism

in a false autonomy. So
if we really are out to monetize
the revolution, to move away
from familiar safe texts
toward innovative
writing, a critical and exploratory

poetics driven
                    by
the innovation that marks private
enterprise, then—what? Partially

dissolved, exhausted—but
doesn't all text feel
manipulated? In a lucid dream we
could redirect
the action; today we're moved along
along wide interstellar
intervals, proper
nouns.
            Invisible like the silent *b*
in debt, it begins sleep or trance…
as a time comes to sweep away

the dust, the individual
granules of crushed stone
that make up the moments

of our attention. Till it strays
off target again, like
nineteenth century prose.

Kolinahr

Ventriloquy, channeling as synonyms. Index a perfect self partly
seen banging on a piano. Or curse as the word discipline has
'unhappy connotations.' Like falling in a purple text, jagged
handwriting as negative voice, eyes mask as wind or whir. Wait
another day, then the nothing gold. The set consists of a mini-hihat,
mini-snare, and a triangular unit with three skins.

Yes, I'm still getting it and even a couple years ago I saw he died
and I still get mail from him.

Yes, you're never more alone than when you improvise. 'The
conscious and intelligent manipulation of the organized habits and
opinions of the masses,' according to Bernays, 'is an important
element in democratic society.'

Be mindful. Remember what you look like. Said they would soon
change the method from the written to the spoken.

Here the blue heron lightly steps looking in dark water for
movement.

As in the mental discipline whereby this state was maintained,
Kolinahr.

Foggy Bottom

Indivisible is the name of a protest movement.
Yes, options can be dangerous.

The mystic chords singingly sonorous but
our future goes like this—we find the metro

to Dupont Circle, right there
is a Krispie Kreme! And the street we need

is the one that spells home, the bus
we have to find has the name

of our destination written on it in big red cursive letters.
Brevity! A 6,000-word brain dump

isn't the most efficient way to sway opinion?
Without risk there is no return.

But it was the closure we needed
easier than writing a spec

for an already existing show
where you can hear how the jokes are staged.

Just our luck, a mad president one tweet away
from starting a nuclear war

sanitized for American audiences
and everywhere those shoes.

These key questions unlock our unlimited
potential. In null space then,

a key like a figure on a page.
Foggy Bottom, our eventual destination.

Without risk there is no return.
Then our doppelgangers, taking the same pills.

And this, the idea of tourists, travelers to the afterlife
avoiding city bridges and

other high places where you can see over the rail.
On our way back, a fog as big as NYC.

Last Days of the Republic

Where we are, out in an atrium, where
the veil is visible but for just one second.

The air's like cotton here and leaves
a trail of ink in a vertical design

parsed on a clean sheet but like space
when there's music or sculpture or dance

(large scale public art) and not just lines
of customers passing

into blissful nonexistence, or waiting
for a future of syncretismatic figurations...

Is this the only printable quote they had?
We're all standing eight, it says, and now

with a fake teleological perspective,
auto-tuning it more, changing the timbre,

part of me that has been quiet a long time
could be made to sound more radio friendly.

Beyond Our Arable Orb

Polished chrome voices angled
rather than curved,

the sound like a word
with a typo in it that turns
      out to be
the number eight—

next the word tertiary
but as an antonym,
the prize articulately tuned in
to what it took
to wreck you here…'Ever get the feeling
you've been cheated?'

The brain is all exteriors now
caught in a space too expertly

(perfectly) measured out in
      a jungle of
           vocabularies full
of floating
          signifiers like the

     moon

RE: Fishing

1

Colleagues: It has begun and it is exciting! The white curve just
now making sharp electrical connections quickens. Certain of a
spiraling future, our eyes get fixed to a shiny opulence.

Tired of owning junk? Insert trendy electronica here. Heed the
commodification of our f***ing souls. As what we started with
dissolves in unless otherwise specified. Where each hour adds
surface texture pulsing on roads leading to where a broken neon
light

brightly speaking in clichés—its fiery century erupts, resets, trees
black and frozen, these days…but we need to stop being the
walking dead. Oligarchy, anyone?

2

You hafta know how the weather affects the water from the point
of view of the fish. Which can see *out* of the water better than you
could see *in*. All it has to do is wait. So you have to cast down
passed it and bring it up on the side so it doesn't have time to react
and it'll hafta take a shot—Is this food? I better

get it, the fish says to himself, and strikes. Re: fishing. I sat with
my back to the hot sun, against my ruin, and read in my devotional
that we are here to serve not question. Leadership is about making
groups more effective. Low-level radiation from flat screen TVs
helps ossify public opinion in accord with benevolent commercial
interests.

Today, they have underwater cameras that literally go down and
find the fish, get 'em on film—and what d' you hafta do after that?

3

Unbendable lines, linguistic shifters
in a cavernous ballroom. A mad pursuit

of the reader of antagonistic glances. The film packed
with heavy-hitters
that boasts some inspired visuals where

all events occur simultaneously but the best you can get
from the earpiece is a homophonic translation
substituting word for word, line for line.

A binary like foxglove, its purified
chemicals referred to as digitoxin.

Creating new exciting worlds cleaves
our consensus,
the lyrics loud enough to diffuse darkness.

The imagined life opulent and serene but
losing its cohesiveness. This in a time of havoc

and deception when the exhausted sun takes up his cycle.

Hints that prayer points a way,
markers of a lost or last crossing.

Crystallizing stunningly obdurate blocks
of polysemic texts, official

court documents. Liberating dreams
to invent new uses for the yet unprocessed.

Where there is no other way to interface,
lyric intimacy's inexorable anacoluthon—

Murk Plectrum

Grab your free "When guns are outlawed,
I'll be an outlaw" T-shirt today!
This is on my bucket list too. Awesome pic!
Taking full responsibility in a handwritten statement
makes it all the more authentic.

Instinctively all the windows reflect towers—
but who's really calling the shots?
A helicopter could zoom in and out of frame—
and we may never know, but the bay
would remain still in a photograph.

A wall projects or delineates a space in open air.
At night it sounds like a splicing of lives
till all the definitions adjust to new settings.
Then that quote from the pope
commenting on the fate of disposable people—

The earth will literally crack open
and would we know if the pattern we followed
is instinct or just borrowed
even as we glide into a new day where
everything cycles endlessly, indelible as graffiti?

Manifesto

Trimming memories, dreamlake—
a wall delineates.
Imagines a poem as a kind of gloss.

The poet's work as a site of divination.
Incessantly destroying
the old, incessantly creating

the new, exact words.
Like ice sculpture, time splashing.
In a world always bending

as one continual fancy. Then
not bending. What proof is *solid mass*
if it's this light it floats on air,

slips through walls? The poet as radio
then, where dictation is
a kind of not-knowing of no-self—

About the Author

David Wyman's first poetry collection *Proletariat Sunrise* was published by Kelsay Books in 2017. He's a fan of Noam Chomsky, jazz guitar, and the visionary poetry of William Blake. He lives in Massachusetts, where he teaches American Literature and writing at Mount Wachusett Community College.

www.ingramcontent.com/pod-product-compliance
Lightning Source LLC
Chambersburg PA
CBHW072048090426
42733CB00033B/2475